Life Lessons from

The Squire and the Scroll

Includes
Squire Ceremony Guide

by Jennie Bishop
with Susan Henson

Companion to the children's storybook *The Squire and the Scroll* by Jennie Bishop
Illustrations from *The Squire and the Scroll* by Preston McDaniels

Published by Revive Our Hearts (an outreach of Life Action Ministries)
P.O. Box 2000, Niles, MI 49120

Illustrations from *The Squire and the Scroll* © 2004 by Warner Press, Anderson, IN.
Illustrated by Preston McDaniels.
All excerpts taken from *The Squire and the Scroll* copyrighted © by Jennie Bishop.
Used by permission. All rights reserved.

Project Manager: Stephen Barnes
Managing Editor: Dawn-Marie Wilson
Layout, design and additional illustrations: David Miles

ISBN: 0-940110-67-9

Printed in the United States of America

Table of Contents

Notes from the Author

After the incredible response to the story of The Princess and the Kiss, *moms everywhere began to ask me, "But what about my son?" Soon* The Squire and the Scroll *was published in answer to those requests.*

And it only makes sense to follow the storybook for boys with a devotional, just as we did in the case of The Princess and the Kiss. *We want to mine the story for the gems of truth from the "Scroll," the holy Word of God, which will equip you and your son to face the challenges of raising or becoming a young man of pure heart and character.*

It isn't too early to teach your son about these issues. Too many of our young squires have been lost for the kingdom because they were ill-prepared for the challenges ahead. Our culture creates an environment where innocence is easily lost at an early age. But it doesn't have to be that way. We can teach our sons how to guard their hearts when they are very young so that when temptation comes they will be able to stand up against it.

Before you begin, please take some time to read through these opening tips. Then, before you begin each lesson, read through the Parents' Compass tips in the back of the book. They aren't really rules, just guidelines. We respect your ability to follow God's leading. Your son is in your home because God knew you were the perfect parent for him!

Blessings to you,
Jennie Bishop, Author
The Squire and the Scroll

How to Use This Book

Relationship, Relationship!

The male ego is fragile. Your son desperately needs your encouragement and a sensitive, listening ear during this study. These topics are tender for him. Make every effort to connect with his heart, not just get the lesson done. Prepare your own heart attitude so your son knows this is a time when your attention is completely his, a time when he is completely safe in sharing his deepest hopes and fears.

Dad, YOU are the most important example your son will ever have, and the time you spend with your son during this study can change his life forever. Don't delegate this responsibility to Mom lightly. The Bible clearly puts you in charge of spiritual instruction. So many young men today suffer because of lack of intimacy with their dads. Don't let your son be one of them! Make the necessary sacrifices to show him that a real man cares enough to prioritize his family.

Our children absorb what we teach, mostly because there is relationship connected with those teachings. Rules without relationship often result in rebellion. In your son's journey from adolescence toward manhood, the battle for purity and integrity may be the greatest battle of his life, and he needs you right now more than ever. If you are not available to teach him these truths, our crooked culture will be more than happy to fill in for you. Don't let that happen! Use these life lessons to equip your son with godly armor that will protect his mind, heart and spirit while in service for his King.

As you begin these lessons, be prepared! Your son may ask some pointed questions and make revealing comments. Be gentle, be sensitive, and listen, listen, listen . . . don't "preach." Discuss the issues at hand openly and in an age-appropriate manner. Open your own heart, too, and be willing for God to strengthen your own sense of purity and integrity.

Read Ahead

Prepare yourself by briefly reading through the material beforehand. There may be stories from your own life that you can share or material that you may want to hold back until your son is ready. Make all your creative edits before you begin the lesson together. The Parents' Compass in the back of this guide will also be helpful in your preparation, giving you extra insight, ideas for discussion, and ways to reinforce the lesson that day.

Our suggestion is that you do one or two life lessons a week with your son, but you can work through the lessons at any pace you like. Just choose a time of day that is peaceful for both of you. If there are scheduling conflicts, be willing to reschedule. Care for your son's immediate needs first and be willing to come back to the lesson later.

Creative Squire Adventures

These creative, interactive ideas will reinforce the lessons of the day. You might want to choose one or two ideas to underscore the lesson and save some adventures for a return trip to that lesson. You may even create adventures of your own as the Lord brings them to mind. Please note that many of these activities require supplies and preparation.

Scriptures

As you study, look up the Scripture references in a version of the Bible that your son seems to comprehend well. He will retain more of what he learns if he understands the vocabulary in the Bible passages.

Read through as many verses as time allows. Memorize the verse from the Scroll of Truth or choose a verse of your own that fits the lesson. Even if your son doesn't seem to remember them for long, each one is a seed planted in his heart, and God promises that those seeds will bear fruit as your son moves toward God-honoring manhood.

Trust God in You

As you move through the different parts of each study, tune in to the Holy Spirit and His leading. God will prompt you with ideas, questions, or personal experiences that He means for you to share. Don't be afraid to be appropriately open about your own shortcomings and weaknesses. You will be amazed at how supportive and open your child becomes when he sees your humility and honesty in sharing. God chose you to lead your son and give him a strong foundation and heritage in His truth, so trust the Lord to lead you.

It isn't too early to teach your son about these important life issues. Remember, everything in the lesson is made to work together for your son's benefit as you respond to God's leadership. God lives in you. His Word is alive and active in you. You can do it!

Special note to moms or single moms leading in this study: You are in good company! Many great men of faith in the Bible and in our society today were shaped by the influence of a godly mom. Trust God to provide all you need as you mentor your son, and do not allow the Enemy to discourage you. Your surrendered life will be a wonderful channel for God to work in your son. You may consider encouraging some male mentors to work with your son on lessons where you feel it would be most helpful.

The Lesson Order

We recommend completing the lessons in the order given, but again, seek God's direction in this. The lesson concepts are appropriate for children of any age, but you know your son best, and you will know when he is ready for certain lessons. After the first six lessons or so, your son should begin to have a good grasp of the material and be able to participate in a Squires of the Lantern Ceremony at any time following.

The "Big Talk"

We chose not to go into details concerning sexual issues but simply to address the importance of purity. However, we recommend that you seek out whatever information you need to feel comfortable to share detailed information as opportunities arise. Don't be timid. Be fearless and clear in presenting the information your child needs to cope with his changing body and emotions.

Your child will hear lots of "facts" from his friends as he grows. But who knows which of those facts will be accurate? Be prepared for pointed questions. Your son needs to know that YOU are the one he can come to for honest answers. Wouldn't you rather he receive your insight than the locker room version? Your testimony about the rewards of obedience and purity will make a deeper impression on your son than any book or film. Be that safe source of information for him. Listen, listen, listen . . . be sensitive and offer helpful information.

The Ceremony

It is so important for young boys to participate in a *rite of passage* ceremony that gives them an opportunity to receive their parents' public, verbal affirmation. The ceremony described in the back of this book is a wonderful event orchestrated to bring families together to bless their sons in a memorable, formal way. The ceremony expresses support and unconditional love, and it can be conducted in a group or simply as a family. We suggest that you set a date for your ceremony as you begin this study. The Ceremony Guide in the back of this book explains all the details.

It's Worth It!

Your little boy is becoming a man before your very eyes. The sacrifice of your schedule that it will take to accomplish these lessons is miniscule compared to the benefits of equipping your son to make a rock-solid stand for Christ. As you complete these devotionals, you can know that you have covered information that will affect and bless your son's life forever. You are working with God, not only to encourage him in his quest toward purity in manhood, but also to pass on a godly heritage to your son and his future family!

So be strong and courageous, Parent, as you encourage your squire to be all he can be for King and kingdom! Be purposeful about preparing and equipping him for the battles ahead. And may he be like the squire in the story, who was not only knighted, but became prince and heir to the father's kingdom.

1. Becoming God's Pure Knight

YOU CAN RISE TO THE CHALLENGE OF MANHOOD BY BEING BRAVE ENOUGH TO DO WHAT'S RIGHT.

A Squire Prepares His Heart

Don't you get excited when you read stories about knights and kings? God designed mankind to rule over the earth (Genesis 1:26), and guess what—you were created to be one of those men! But *ruling* doesn't just require power. It takes courage, honor, loyalty and a strong spirit. The greatest kings and knights (and husbands and fathers) are those who serve and protect others (Mark 10:43-45). They are men who are not afraid to stand up for what is right, even when no one else does (Daniel 3:16-18). Those men are true heroes!

The first words in the story of *The Squire and the Scroll* are, "In the days when men of valor still guarded kings...." *Valor* is another word for bravery or courage. As Joshua prepared to lead the Israelites into the Promised Land, God said three different times, "Be strong and courageous" (Joshua 1:6-9). God told Joshua to be a man of valor.

As you begin your quest toward purity and integrity in adulthood, God is saying the same thing to you: "_____ (put your name in the blank), be strong and courageous!" He wants you to stand up for what is right and to keep your heart pure, even when no one else does. When you obey God's Word, just as the squire in the story obeyed the words of the scroll, you will become a true knight in God's kingdom—a man of courage and valor!

A Squire's Prayer

Lord, I bow before You as my King. Prepare me to become Your knight by filling my heart with a sincere desire to know Your Word. Teach me how to trust You and Your Word so I will do what is right, no matter what my friends are doing. Help me become courageous like Joshua, Lord! I pray in Jesus' name, amen.

Scroll of Truth

"Be on your guard; stand firm in the faith; be men of courage; be strong."

1 Corinthians 16:13

Creative Squire Adventures

A Courageous Heart—Are there activities you would like to do but may not feel quite brave enough to try? Talk to your parents about one activity you would like to try, but you need their encouragement. Your mom or dad will cheer you on, and you'll feel great as you act bravely and overcome your fears!

Marks of Valor—Look up the words *valor*, *chivalry*, and *integrity*. On the left-hand side of a piece of paper, make a list of words describing a man of character. On the opposite side, list some negative character traits that would not make someone a hero or a knight. Now create some ribbons of valor out of construction paper or wide ribbon. With a marker, write each trait of a hero on a separate ribbon. Each day have a parent select one of the ribbons to show a good character trait you modeled that day.

Hero of the Faith: Joshua

Read Joshua 1. What did Joshua have to do that might have seemed scary? What happened when he was obedient? How is Joshua a hero?

Battle Plans

Some heroes have money, success, or popularity, but their lives are full of sin. How can sin ruin the life of a potential hero—and the lives of others around him?

Can you remember a time when you needed courage? Are there any parts of growing up that make you feel like you need more courage?

2. Choosing to Serve the King

TO BECOME GOD'S KNIGHT, YOU MUST DECIDE TO SERVE YOUR KING—JESUS.

A Squire Prepares His Heart

The first requirement of a knight is that he remains faithful, trustworthy and obedient to his king. The squire in the story decided to "serve the good king" with all his heart. He practiced this by being a faithful servant to the knight who was his master.

In your life you will have to decide whom you will serve. Each time you make a decision, you are choosing whether you will do what *you* want to do or what your Master, *Jesus*, wants you to do.

Jesus is the best example of a servant who ever lived. Everything He did was done because it was what His Father wanted (John 5:19). Because Jesus was obedient and faithful, He received a name above all names (Philippians 2:5-9).

Obedience means that you will give up the right to act as you please in order to pursue what God wants. You will allow Jesus to live through you (Galatians 2:20). Have you given your life to Jesus in this way? If you choose to serve Jesus as King of your heart, He will live in you and through you, giving you power to become the valiant knight He has always meant you to be. If you have never asked Jesus to be your King and Savior, now is the time!

A Squire's Prayer

Jesus, will You sit on the throne in my heart and rule there as my King? Forgive me for wanting to do things only for myself. Give me a heart that wants to serve You more than anything else. Thank You, Jesus. Amen.

Scroll of Truth

"Choose for yourselves this day whom you will serve. . . . But as for me and my household, we will serve the LORD."

Joshua 24:15

Creative Squire Adventures

An Honorable Quest—Imagine the King giving you a mission to accomplish this week—a special task to serve someone in need. Find someone who needs your help and remember that you are serving King Jesus as you serve that person. If asked why you are serving, say, "For King and kingdom!" and explain how you are serving Jesus.

Seeker Expedition—Write out the Scroll of Truth verse (Joshua 24:15) on 3x5 cards, one word per card. Write a second set in a different color. Have someone hide the cards around the room. Race with a parent or friend to find all the cards and put them in order. Play the game several times this week.

Hero of the Faith: Abraham

Read Genesis 22:1-19. Abraham was willing to give up what he loved most because he wanted to obey God. What was the sacrifice he was willing to make? What did God do because Abraham was willing to be obedient?

Battle Plans

The squire made sacrifices in service. He left his family, made a long and difficult trip, and served his master instead of himself. What are some difficult things you may have to do or give up as you serve King Jesus?

Why should we serve Jesus as our King? Just because we have to? Or is there another reason? Why is it important to decide whom you will serve?

3. Reaching Dreams God Has Given You

GOD HAS A SPECIFIC, WONDERFUL PLAN FOR YOUR LIFE— A JOB THAT HE WANTS YOU TO DO.

A Squire Prepares His Heart

In medieval times some fathers and sons worked hard to follow the "Knight's Code of Conduct." A knight was to be courageous, loyal, faithful, honest, obedient, pure, gracious and forgiving. He would be gentle and courteous around young ladies. He would face temptations with confidence. He knew what to do in every challenge because he was focused on the "code," and he wanted to please the king. Any boy who wanted to be a knight would need to mirror the Knight's Code in his attitudes and conduct.

The young man in *The Squire and the Scroll* knew the words of his scroll so well that he even dreamed about them. He studied them and kept them in his heart because he knew they were the keys to making his dream of knighthood come true.

God has a very good, specific plan for your life (Jeremiah 29:11), an amazing adventure. He planted deep in your heart a special dream to fulfill that plan. God makes it clear that we must read, study, memorize and *remember* His Word to receive the gifts He promises us (Joshua 1:8).

The squire's dream was to become a knight. What dream has God given to you? (What sounds exciting to you? Do you like to work with machines? Do you like to explore, write, cook, study or build things?) When you accomplish God's dream for you, you will bring Him glory (Colossians 3:23-34). God wants to make you strong to accomplish those dreams (2 Chronicles 16:9a).

A Squire's Prayer

Thank You, God, for giving me special dreams that will come true as I allow You to work through me. Help me know Your Word so well that I always think about it and live by its truth. I will follow and obey You so I can become the knight You made me to be. Amen.

Scroll of Truth

"'For I know the plans I have for you,' declares the LORD, 'plans to prosper you and not to harm you, plans to give you hope and a future.'" Jeremiah 29:11

Creative Squire Adventures

Silversmith Skills—Wrap and glue heavy-duty aluminum foil around a large piece of cardboard that is cut into the shape of a cross. Using a ballpoint pen, make designs that include words like *loyalty*, *courage*, and *integrity* (look up these words if you're not sure what they mean). Put the words "GOD'S KNIGHT" on the cross somewhere in big letters. Hang the cross in your room to remind you of the goal you're reaching for every day.

Hiding the Word—Write Psalm 119:11 on an index card. Put it in your shirt or pants pocket and carry it to school. Read it often, especially if you are tempted to be unkind or disobedient. The hidden Word in your pocket will soon become the hidden Word in your heart, making you more like a pure knight every time you read it!

Hero of the Faith: Joseph

Talk about the story of Joseph (Genesis 37:5-11). What dream did God give to Joseph? Was he wise to share the dream with his brothers? What might have happened to Joseph's dreams if he had not set his mind to live by God's rules?

Battle Plans

Sinful living can wreck our dreams. What good choices can you make now to protect your dreams for the future?

Think of some answers you can give when friends tempt you to do what's wrong. How and when will you say *no*?

4. Protecting Your Purity

Your purity is a treasure to be guarded and kept safe.

A Squire Prepares His Heart

When we give our lives to Jesus, our bodies become a home for the Holy Spirit (1 Corinthians 3:16). God lives in us. We are like a jar of clay where a wonderful, holy treasure is kept (2 Corinthians 4:7). We are responsible to keep our lives clean!

The Lantern of Purest Light in *The Squire and the Scroll* represented purity in the kingdom. When it was stolen, all the people suffered.

The gift of purity was given to you on the day you were born. It is a precious treasure that God wants you to value for your entire life.

Keeping your heart pure means you are willing to guard what comes into your life through the doors of your senses. It means making wise choices about what you watch, read, eat, touch, and even smell (Proverbs 4:20-27). If you allow dirt to come into your life through impure song lyrics or movies with ungodly images, you won't be able to live freely and joyfully, as God intended.

The squire in the story made good choices during each stage of his quest. Remember when he covered his eyes with the shield? You can do the same! Learn to guard the "doors of your heart"—your five senses. Fight hard! Don't let the Enemy steal any part of your purity. Then you will be a "house" fit for your King, and you will also stay pure for the woman you may someday marry.

A Squire's Prayer

Father, I know there are all kinds of dirt in the world that can make my heart unclean. I want You to feel at home in my life. Show me how to make good decisions every day that keep my "house" a wonderful, clean place for You to live. Amen.

Scroll of Truth

"Above all else, guard your heart, for it is the wellspring of life."

Proverbs 4:23

16

Creative Squire Adventures

Guarding the Light—Build a campfire or take a candle outside at night. What must be done to keep the fire or the candle lit? Talk about what kinds of wind might "blow out" a person's light of purity. What might happen if we choose to live in the darkness? What are some rewards of guarding the light of purity? How can Jesus restore any light that is lost and bring forgiveness when we sin? (See 1 John 1:5-9.)

Family Flashlight Tag—You will need one flashlight. Choose a tagger. Everyone runs and hides in the dark while the tagger counts. The goal is to tag people out by shining the light on each person before he or she tags you on the back. The first person tagged out with the light is the next tagger.

Hero of the Faith: Solomon

Who is the wisest person you know? The wisest man who ever lived, King Solomon, wanted his son to understand the importance of purity. In Proverbs 7:1-5, Solomon taught his son the Word of God. He told him to stay away from any woman who would tempt him to sin by becoming impure. Solomon wanted his son to keep himself pure for the wife God might give him some day. Solomon told his son to write God's laws of wisdom on his heart, which means to remember what God says. Are you writing God's words of wisdom on your heart?

Battle Plans

In the story, the Lantern of Purest Light was stolen. How can purity be stolen? Name the five ways the squire guarded his purity in the story. Can you think of a way you can guard each one of your five senses to keep your heart clean?

Some people think it's cool to get into trouble, and that impure actions make a man more manly. How would you answer someone who felt this way? Why does it sometimes take courage to protect your purity?

How can you set a good example for your friends in matters of purity without being mean? What if you have a friend who listens to music with filthy lyrics, or a buddy who talks about girls and their bodies in an unclean, disrespectful way?

5. Accepting the Protection of Authority

ALLOWING YOUR PARENTS OR OTHERS IN AUTHORITY TO PROTECT AND GUIDE YOU WILL HELP YOU BECOME A WISE YOUNG MAN.

A Squire Prepares His Heart

Remember the part of *The Squire and the Scroll* when the young man leaves home? Look at that picture again, if you can. His parents seem to be very happy about his send-off. They're not glad he's leaving, but they're so proud of him. You can tell that they trust him to be successful in his quest. They've done their best to teach him from the scroll and to remind him that they will always support him in his quest for the king (Deuteronomy 6:6-7).

Parents aren't perfect, but if a parent or guardian is going through this book with you, you can know that he (or she) cares very much about teaching you to guard your heart and your purity. They are eager for your success in this great adventure with God.

Many sons disrespect their parents and others in authority. Popular TV programs and songs often tempt us to believe that children know better than their parents. Don't be tempted to believe these lies! God gave us authorities to teach and protect us. In the Ten Commandments God says to honor your parents. If you do, your life will be blessed (Exodus 20:12).

Why should you respect your parents? They gave you the great gift of life, and God knew they had exactly what you need to grow in wisdom and maturity. If you listen, obey, and honor them—even when they seem strict—you will become a man of character like the squire, ready for a grand adventure with your parents' blessing! (See Proverbs 2:1-11.)

A Squire's Prayer

Lord, guard me against the temptation to dishonor my mom and dad. Give me a deep love for them and a desire to obey. I want my life's adventure to be blessed, so I want to avoid the traps of sin that could ruin my life. I want to be a man of character. Help me honor my parents. Amen.

Scroll of Truth

"Honor your father and your mother, so that you may live long in the land the LORD your God is giving you."

Exodus 20:12

18

Creative Squire Adventures

Guarding Your Heart—Play a simple game of soccer or kickball with your parents (your siblings or a friend can join you). Mark off a large playing area in a gym or outside, in the size you think is best. Give your dad or mom the job of guarding you. Let another person (or the other parent) try to tag you by kicking the ball. When your "guarding" parent is successful in guarding you, you get points. Talk about how this works in real life. If you don't guard your heart, who gets the points?

Keys to a Clean Life—Some day, when you get a car of your own, you will make many life choices. If you want freedom later, you need to prove every day while you are younger that you are a wise decision-maker. Draw and cut out four large car keys. On each key write out one verse of Psalm 119:9-11, 30. Place the keys in your room to remind you that you must be careful to live according to God's Word and seek His direction.

Heroes of the Faith: Ham, Shem, and Japheth

We often hear about Noah and the ark, but what about Noah's sons? In Genesis 6:9-14, 18, and 7:1, we discover that Noah built a huge wooden ship to save his family from a worldwide flood of judgment. Noah's sons probably helped him in this huge task that took 120 years! They believed Noah's words and honored his relationship with God. God saved Noah's family from destruction. Do you think Noah taught his sons about the Lord when they were young? Genesis 9:1 says that God blessed Noah and his sons. Do you think that honoring your parents and letting God use them in your life will bring you blessing?

Battle Plans

What keeps you from giving your heart to your parents for safekeeping (Proverbs 23:26)? If there is any need in your heart or in your parents' hearts to seek forgiveness, talk gently about it; ask God for forgiveness and healing, and then forgive each other, as necessary. Son, ask God to help you trust your parents' wisdom and protection. Parent, ask God to help you listen and be open and understanding.

What are some things your parents have done that remind you of how much they care about you and your future?

What are some ways that you can respect and honor your parents today?

6. Living by the Scroll

GOD'S WORD KEEPS YOU ON THE RIGHT PATH IN YOUR QUEST TO BECOMING A KNIGHT FOR HIM.

A Squire Prepares His Heart

Knowing the Bible—your Scroll—will help you recognize any advice that doesn't sound like what you've learned from God, your parents and other authorities (Acts 17:11).

Hiding God's Word in our hearts (Psalm 119:11, 30) takes some work. Hearing people read the Bible at church or Sunday school is good, but it's also important to study, memorize and remember it on your own. Bible verses are like seeds that grow in your life. Once they're planted they bring good fruit like love, joy, peace and patience into your life (Galatians 5:22-23).

The squire could say all the truths of the scroll by heart. He even dreamed about them! He kept the scroll at his side at all times. The knight didn't remember the rules on the scroll, so he couldn't follow them very well. The same is true in your life. Knowing God's Word will prepare you for anything that's ahead and lead you in becoming a knight for the Lord.

Your friends' feelings about what is right or wrong may change because they may not know God's truth (Psalm 33:4). But God's Word never changes. Always ask, "What does the Bible say?" (Proverbs 12:15), so you can recognize the lies of the Enemy. The Word of God is powerful!

A Squire's Prayer

Father, please give me a love for Your Word, and help me understand and remember what I read. I want my heart to be good ground for the seed of Your Word so my life will be full of good fruit! When I am faced with choices, remind me to ask, "What does the Bible say?" Help me do what is right and pure. Amen.

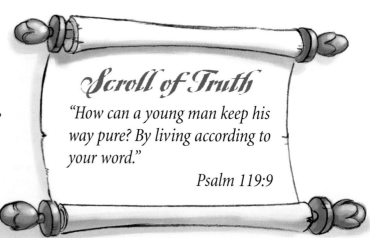

Scroll of Truth

"How can a young man keep his way pure? By living according to your word."

Psalm 119:9

20

Creative Squire Adventures

"Sword of the Spirit" Challenge—You will need two wrapping paper rolls (cardboard tubes). On each roll, write "The Sword of the Spirit, which is the Word of God." On the other side of the first roll, write Psalm 119:9. On the other side of the second roll, write Psalm 33:4. Memorize your verses. For a Sword Battle, each person takes a turn reciting their verse. With each word in the verse, they get a free blow to their opponent's sword, while the opponent stands in defense. (Swing only at the sword, not at the person.)

Nickel Sword Drill—The son begins with 25 nickels ($1.25). Give him 20 seconds to find a specified verse in the Bible. (Perhaps use specific verses from this study.) If he finds the verse and begins to read it before the 20 seconds are up, he gets to keep his nickels. Each time he can't find the verse in the specified time, he loses a nickel. (If your child is unfamiliar with the Bible, you may want to have him find a book of the Bible in 20 seconds, or change the length of time instead.)

Hero of the Faith: Josiah

A wonderful story about Josiah is found in 2 Chronicles 34. Josiah was only eight years old when he became a king. His father was not a godly example, but Josiah the king "began to seek [after] God," "not turning aside to the right or to the left." Josiah also tore down all the statues of false gods in the land. He lived for God even when others did not. What did Josiah do when he found out that he and his people had not fully obeyed God's law? How did his action make him a heroic king and leader? How can your choices to stand for God's truths help to change your generation?

Battle Plans

Josiah and the squire each made a personal decision at an early age to follow God's ways even when others did not. Have you made that decision?

Why do some young men not take God's Word seriously, or think it is "cool" not to pray? How does the decision to obey the Lord show courage and strong character?

7. Guarding Your Ears

WHAT COMES INTO YOUR HEART THROUGH YOUR EARS CAN MAKE A DIFFERENCE IN HOW YOU LIVE.

A Squire Prepares His Heart

The squire understood that his five senses were like doors that opened into his heart and spirit (Proverbs 4:20-27). When he and the knight passed through the enchanted forest, the squire knew from studying the scroll that he must close his ears and only listen to words that were pure. Any evil that entered his ears would end up in his mind and possibly his actions!

Battles are fought and won in the heart and mind. The Word of God is like a guard standing watch at the door of your mind; it will remind you to think only pure thoughts (Philippians 4:8). When impure thoughts come, a mind filled with God's Word says, "You don't belong here!"

There are many ways that impurity can enter your mind. Would the words in music that you or your friends listen to hurt God's heart or offend others? Turn off or throw away any dirt that can clog up your heart. If you are with friends, walk away or politely explain what you believe and why. Maybe they've never thought about guarding their own ears. Dirty jokes, cursing, and gossip about others are also not for you (Ephesians 4:29). Walk away, or try to turn the conversation around with a clean joke or positive comment (Colossians 4:5-6).

Don't be fooled by the lies of the Enemy. Fortune telling, palm reading, and trying to talk to people who have died isn't just for fun. It's rebellion against God, and it's another open door to sin (1 Samuel 15:23a; Deuteronomy 18:10-12a). You have been set aside to do God's work, so guard all of your senses against evil (Ephesians 5:3-4).

A Squire's Prayer

Lord, it's so easy to be affected by unclean words. Make me the kind of man who refuses to listen to filthy talk. Give me the discipline I need to turn off songs or programs that fill my ears with anything unclean. Thank You, Lord. Amen.

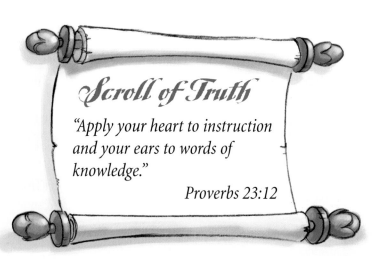

Scroll of Truth

"Apply your heart to instruction and your ears to words of knowledge."

Proverbs 23:12

Creative Squire Adventures

All Ears!—Music with unclean words affects people even if they're not listening to the words. Have your parent(s) bring out a few of their favorite CDs, and you get a few of yours. Pick a song from each CD that you like, and tell whether the artist honors God in the music and lyrics. Be honest with each other and before the Lord. Is there anything—music or otherwise—that doesn't belong in your home? Ask God to help you do the right thing.

"Hear ye! Hear ye!" Helmet Night—Purchase a helmet (or special hat) to focus on guarding the ears. Write or attach the reference Philippians 4:8 on the helmet. Catch family members saying or listening to things that bless others—including using words like *please* and *thank you*, complimenting or praising someone, or playing uplifting Christian music. If someone says or listens to something good, they get to wear the helmet and catch the next person!

Hero of the Faith: Samuel

In 1 Samuel 3:1-11 we read that Samuel heard God's voice. Why did Samuel have trouble knowing who was calling him the first time, in verse seven? Why is this important? Samuel returned to Eli again and again, longing to obey his call. How did his desire to listen and obey develop him into a hero later? (See Psalm 99:6.)

Battle Plans

Read 1 Corinthians 10:12-13. What are some ways of escape that God can provide when you are faced with temptation? (See Proverbs 30:5.)

Why do we need to guard our imaginations and our ears? Read Jeremiah 7:23-24.

What does God say about those who listen to wrong speech? (See Proverbs 17:4.)

8. Guarding Your Eyes

YOU MUST CONTROL WHAT COMES INTO YOUR HEART AND LIFE THROUGH YOUR EYES.

A Squire Prepares His Heart

We live in a world full of evil images like the ones on the tunnel walls in *The Squire and the Scroll*. The wise, healthy, godly man will choose not to look at evil (Psalm 101:3). As a young man you must learn to *master* (control) your eyes, because you will certainly be tempted in this way. Genesis 4:7 says, ". . . sin is crouching [lying in wait] at your door; it desires to have you, but you must master [rule over] it."

You can guard your eyes by turning off anything on TV that wouldn't please Jesus. (Ask, "Would Jesus be laughing along or shedding tears?") If your family attends movies, check movie reviews and ratings with your parent(s) before you go.

Some reading materials have pictures and articles that can pull you into sin. It is never right to look at pictures of women who are not fully clothed (Proverbs 6:25-29). This dishonors women and steals away your character. Enjoying each other's bodies is a gift from God meant to be shared between a man and woman in marriage. God never meant for people to uncover so much of their bodies in front of others.

Turn your eyes away from billboards, store window displays, CD covers, video games, movies and magazines that do not please God. If you don't, you will develop a habit of looking that leads into darkness. Looking on evil images is not the way to become a man. A true man of honor, respect and integrity will raise his shield to protect his eyes and keep his heart pure for God, his wife and his family (Proverbs 17:24).

A Squire's Prayer

Dear God, there are so many impure things in this world. When those things come into my sight, help me to turn away and think about You and Your Word. You created me for greatness in Your kingdom, and I need to carefully guard my heart. Keep me from temptation, and help me to choose what is right. Amen.

Scroll of Truth

"Turn my eyes away from worthless things; preserve my life according to your word."
Psalm 119:37

Creative Squire Adventures

Shield or Catch—Find a trash can lid or a large tray to use as a shield (ask permission first). Then have your parent toss some soft foam balls at you. The person who throws the balls also calls out things that eyes can see. If the example is good, catch the ball. If not, use your shield! (For example: An ocean view would be good, but certain TV programs would be bad.)

See No Evil—How did the second rule of the scroll provide a way of escape for the squire? Write out Psalm 101:3a and ask permission to tape it to your TV or video games for the week. Or, write out Proverbs 4:25 and tape this verse to a pair of sunglasses. Set the sunglasses in your room as a reminder to guard your eyes.

Hero of the Faith: Joseph

Joseph was a man of wisdom and strong character. The Bible describes how he did the right thing when tempted to look at Potiphar's wife impurely (Genesis 39:6b-12). The secret of not falling into sinful "eye traps" is in Psalm 25:14-15. How did Joseph follow the wisdom found in this psalm? What was the focus of his eyes? David, another one of our heroes, made a terrible mistake when he allowed his eyes to wander (2 Samuel 11:1-5). Although God loved David and forgave him, there were serious consequences to his sin—consequences that Joseph did not have to face because he wisely guarded his eyes.

Battle Plans

What are some things that are good to look at? What are some things that aren't so good? Be specific and ask for your parent's help.

How might choosing to guard your eyes now affect your marriage relationship, if God chooses for you to marry some day?

When it comes to protecting your eyes from impurity, what might be the consequences of not quickly obeying God?

9. Choosing Friends Wisely

CHOOSE CLOSE FRIENDS WHO WILL ENCOURAGE YOU TO BE MORE LIKE JESUS.

A Squire Prepares His Heart

When the squire became the knight's right-hand man, he may not have had a choice. It may be that he was assigned to the knight. Later, in the cave of jewels, he found that the knight was not a godly example. The knight's pride and the lust of his eyes kept him from obedience. Happily, the squire knew how to practice what he believed, even when the knight didn't.

You have a choice about who you hang around with. The Bible tells us that bad company can tempt a good man to make poor choices (1 Corinthians 15:33). Our friends can have a big effect on us. If they act proud then we'll be tempted to be proud too. If they think only sissies cry then we'll be tempted to stuff our feelings and make fun of others who are hurting. If they tell dirty jokes or laugh at filthy language, we'll be tempted to go along with the crowd. Spending time with boys like this is not wise (Proverbs 24:1-2).

If you choose wisely you will surround yourself with good Christian friends who stand for what is right, respect young women, and help others who are weaker (Ecclesiastes 4:12). They will encourage you, not make fun of you (Ecclesiastes 4:9-10). These kinds of friends are respected by those in authority (Proverbs 22:11).

Sometimes there may be only a few friends to choose from, but it's worth it to choose carefully. Pray and be patient. God will help you find godly friends who will encourage you to be more like Jesus!

A Squire's Prayer

Lord Jesus, I need friends who will help me make good choices and encourage me to be like You . . . friends I can trust who won't make fun of me. Show me how to make good choices in friends, and make me a good example to my friends too. Thank You for being my best friend. Amen.

Scroll of Truth

"Do not be misled: 'Bad company corrupts good character.'"

1 Corinthians 15:33

26

Bad Company—Read these passages in Proverbs. Make a list of the things bad friends do. Then on the opposite side of the page make a list of the things that good friends would do instead. (Proverbs 3:31; 22:24-25; 23:12, 20, 22; 24:1, 21; 31:8-9.)

What to Say?—Do some role playing with a parent. Have your parent think of something a tough guy at school might say to embarrass or challenge you. Work together to think of answers that will let him know you stand strong, without making him angry or embarrassing him in return.

Heroes of the Faith: David and Jonathan

David and Jonathan set a great example of friendship. Read 1 Samuel 20:1-16. What did Jonathan want to do for David? Why? What do you think are some of the things that made their friendship so strong?

Battle Plans

How did the knight make it clear he was not a godly example to the squire?

What are the qualities of a good friend?

How can you encourage others at school who are teased or bullied?

10. Guarding Your Mouth

YOU CAN MAKE GOOD CHOICES ABOUT HOW YOU USE YOUR TONGUE AND WHAT GOES INTO YOUR MOUTH.

A Squire Prepares His Heart

One of the hardest parts of the body to control is the tongue. Words can hurt others and cause great pain (Proverbs 11:9a). A godly knight would not want to tell lies or gossip about others, and he would be careful not to quarrel or grumble. A pure knight certainly would not want to speak filthy language. The third rule of the scroll was, "Keep the unclean far from your lips to guard the wellspring of your life." James 3:8 tells us that the tongue is rebellious and hard for us to tame. If it is allowed full, unguarded freedom, its "deadly poison" may pour out and destroy our relationships and every part of our lives.

We may have a tough time guarding our tongue, but God is the source of all wisdom and power, and He can control any part of our bodies. Ask the Lord to guard your tongue (Psalm 141:3). Seek to please Him with every word (Psalm 19:14).

We also need to be careful about what goes between our lips as food. God wants us to be wise about our food choices, and to eat in a balanced way to protect our health. In our culture, where everything is super-sized, it's easy to overeat. Proverbs warns us not to spend time with gluttons—those who won't stop at enough (Proverbs 23:20). So set a guard at your mouth. Watch what you say and what you eat!

A Squire's Prayer

Jesus, I want to be more careful about how I use my tongue. Teach me how to speak only those words that will encourage and bless others. I want to glorify You in all things, so help me practice self-control and make wise, healthy food choices too. Amen.

Scroll of Truth

"Put away perversity [false and dishonest speech] from your mouth; keep corrupt [rebellious] talk far from your lips."
                                    Proverbs 4:24

Creative Squire Adventures

Guard Your Big Mouth—On a large poster board, draw and cut out a big mouth. Write Psalm 141:3 at the top. Parents, toss paper balls into the opening while your son guards it with a plastic bat. Discuss verses about the tongue whenever he fails to guard the Big Mouth.

Meals Fit for a Knight—Help your mom plan and prepare the family meals this week. Choose a healthy, balanced menu. Talk about ways you can make wise choices at school in the lunch line. If you stay afterward for practices, how can you make better choices if you pack snacks or use the vending machines?

Hero of the Faith: Daniel

In Daniel 1:1-20 we see that Daniel must have had amazing self-control. Just think of all the wonderful things the king could have offered him to eat! But Daniel said, "No thank you; just vegetables, please." Why? Daniel chose his words carefully so he would not dishonor the king, while still standing strong for the Lord. How did his words and self-control show God's power to everyone? How did God bless Daniel and his friends?

Battle Plans

What struggles do you have with your tongue? Lying? Gossiping? Filthy talk? Pray today with your parents about this struggle.

Can you think of one thing you eat that is not healthy? How can you limit this food or eliminate it completely?

II. Guarding Your Hands and Feet

YOU CAN MAKE GOOD CHOICES WITH YOUR HANDS AND FEET—WHAT YOU TOUCH AND WHERE YOU GO.

A Squire Prepares His Heart

The squire was careful about what he touched. Remember when he cautioned the knight not to touch the gems in the stone walls? We can use our hands for good or evil (Psalm 18:24). We must keep all personal touch safely tucked away as a gift for the wife God may one day provide. We never want to dishonor others or our own bodies.

We also make choices about what is valuable when we gather our possessions. If we constantly use our hands to grab many possessions, we may value them more than people. But there are good ways to use our hands. We can shake hands with a friend, give a hug to our relatives, serve the Lord with our skills and talents, and open our Bibles!

And what about our feet? They can lead away from God if we don't make wise choices. The squire used the scroll to discover the right direction to go. God wants to direct your path, too (Proverbs 3:5-6). All paths have rewards or consequences. We can choose to walk on solid ground by reading and obeying the Word of God (Proverbs 3:6, 23; 4:11-12). We can walk in safe places when we surround ourselves with godly friends. We can avoid the slippery mud of places where we might get into trouble (Proverbs 4:26-27).

Remember: A knight of honor has clean hands and a pure heart (Psalm 24:3-5), and he walks on the right paths (Psalm 119:128).

A Squire's Prayer

Father, I want to use my hands, feet and sense of touch to glorify You in all I do. I know I'll face temptations in my life, and I want to face those times with the courage to do what's right, no matter how I feel. Remind me to go to Your Scroll so You can lead me. Amen.

Scroll of Truth

"Lean not on your own understanding; in all your ways acknowledge him, and he will make your paths straight."

Proverbs 3:5b-6

Creative Squire Adventures

<u>Smart Touch</u>—Have a parent blindfold you and put things into your hands. See if you can tell what they are just by touching them. Talk about your sense of touch and how it can be helpful or hurtful.

<u>The Right Path</u>—Have a parent blindfold you and take you for a barefoot walk outside without giving you direction. How can you tell where the sidewalk is? The grass? A stony driveway? Walking on stones can hurt your feet. How might your spirit hurt if you choose to walk on a dangerous spiritual path? Now let your parent's words direct you. Isn't it easier? God's words will direct you too!

Hero of the Faith: Joseph

Talk about the story of Joseph (Genesis 39:1-12). How did he choose wisely regarding Potiphar's wife and his sense of touch? What did he do with his feet? Joseph later had a wife named Asenath. How do you think she felt about the choice Joseph made in this story?

Battle Plans

What are some places you'd like to visit that are on a right path? What places would be the wrong path?

What things do you hold onto tightly? Are they of true value? Can you share things easily?

What kind of touch would be appropriate when a young man is politely greeting a young lady?

12. Serving the King with Every Breath

YOU CAN CHOOSE TO LIVE FOR YOUR LORD AND KING, WHO GIVES YOU EVERY BREATH.

A Squire Prepares His Heart

When God made man He breathed life into him—it was the very breath of God (Genesis 2:7). Your breath is a gift from God too! (See Isaiah 42:5.)

Did you know that you don't belong to yourself? God says, "You are not your own" (1 Corinthians 6:19). Just as a knight is responsible to loyally obey his king, some day we will stand before God and give an account to Him of our lives on earth (Romans 14:11-12). Wouldn't you like to hear, "Well done, good and faithful servant!" on that day? (See Matthew 25:21.)

When the squire breathed in the pure fragrance of the flower, he passed unharmed through the dangerous smoke and caves. The squire models for us that we must daily turn away from sin and ask to be filled with the Holy Spirit. As we "breathe" Him in, we trust God to give us power and wisdom to do His will and live holy lives in this wicked world.

God has given you life and breath to do His good work on earth. Try to speak the truth about who He is to as many people as you can. Go all out for God, holding nothing back as you work for Him, knowing that nothing you do for King Jesus will ever be a waste of time or effort (1 Corinthians 15:58). Best of all, you can use your breath to sing, praise Him and give Him glory (Psalm 150:6).

And while we're talking about breath, be careful not to harm your breathing and health with cigarettes or any other poisons. Satan would love to destroy you that way, but God wants you to guard your breath and keep your body strong for years to come (Proverbs 3:7-8).

A Squire's Prayer

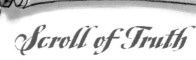

Lord, thank You for the gift of life. I'm so glad to be alive and serving You. I was created to obey You and enjoy You forever. Give me wisdom and fill me with Your Spirit so that some day I will hear You say, "Well done!" Help me to remember that I belong to You. Amen.

Scroll of Truth

"You are not your own; you were bought at a price. Therefore honor God with your body."
1 Corinthians 6:19b-20

Creative Squire Adventures

Big Breath Race—You'll need six cotton balls and a long table. Two players each take three cotton balls. Mark the cotton balls so each player will know which are his. Stand at opposite ends of a long table. Each player tries to blow his first cotton ball off the end of the opponent's side. (If your cotton ball goes off the sides you have to start it over again.) You can blow back your opponent's cotton ball by moving around the table, but be careful because he'll be trying to blow yours back too! The object is to be the first to get your three cotton balls over the opposite side. Talk about God's gift of breath to you and how you can use it in powerful ways for Him.

Psalmist for a Day—Write your own psalm (song) about God's goodness or power. It doesn't have to rhyme . . . David's songs didn't. Sing your psalm to God. Use your breath to praise Him with a whisper, or shout your joyful praises to the Lord!

Hero of the Faith: David

Read Psalms 148 and 150. David wrote many psalms (songs) like these, and he probably sang them when he played on his harp for grumpy King Saul (1 Samuel 16:21-23). David says in Psalm 150:6, "Let everything that has breath praise the LORD." How can you glorify God with your breath, even if you are not a musician or great singer?

Battle Plans

Are you living completely for King Jesus? Does He control your life?

What three things can you do with your breath that would please God?

Why is it important to guard what you breathe into your body?

13. Reaching Out to the Weak

YOU CAN BECOME A COMPASSIONATE MAN, CARING FOR PEOPLE LIKE JESUS DOES. JESUS IS NEVER TOO PROUD TO HELP THE WEAK.

A Squire Prepares His Heart

Pride is a dangerous enemy. Proud men are so full of their own plans and importance they don't have time or patience for anyone else. The squire was an honorable young man, full of warmth and compassion. When he saw the men who had been turned to stone, his heart was touched because he knew that he could have made the same poor decision himself.

You will see men of stone in your life's journey too—people who are often miserable because they do not know about God yet, or men who know God but are not obeying His Word. You can choose to ignore those people or laugh or gossip about them; or you can respect and encourage them (Proverbs 24:11). Share the good news of Christ with them. Help them do what's right, and love them in spite of their weaknesses (1 Thessalonians 5:14-15). God loves each one of them as much as He loves you, and you show that you belong to God by loving them with God's love (1 John 4:20-21).

Are you a popular person who avoids people who are different? Or are you a friend to everyone, willing to reach out to help and bless others?

Feeling compassion for others isn't a sissy thing. It takes a strong man, a man after God's own heart, to feel compassion for those in trouble. Sometimes it takes courage to be kind. Jesus took time for those who were hurting. He was never "too good" to help them. You can be that kind of man—a loving, compassionate and humble friend.

A Squire's Prayer

Father, sometimes I don't show compassion. Please forgive me, and fill my heart with Your compassion so I can help those who are lost and hurting. Many of my friends may never be able to go through a book like this with their parents. They may not even know who You are! Help me tell them about You, Lord. Amen.

Scroll of Truth

"What does the LORD require of you? To act justly and to love mercy and to walk humbly with your God."

Micah 6:8

Creative Squire Adventures

Rescuing the Weak—Read Psalm 41:1-4. Make a list of the blessings that come to a person who is kind to those weaker than himself. Make a plan, with your parents' help, to show kindness today or tomorrow to someone who is weak (perhaps a neighbor or a friend at school).

Strength to Do Right—Stage a Family Arm Wrestling Tournament. Who was the strongest? Discuss: What is strength for? Is it only for winning contests? What's the difference between spiritual strength and physical strength? Read Mark 12:30. How can we show that kind of love?

Hero of the Faith: The Good Samaritan

Read Luke 10:25-37. The Samaritan showed great kindness to an injured man. Did he know the man? Why did he take time to care for this man? What things did he do that may have been dangerous, inconvenient or expensive? Does the Samaritan remind you of anyone you know?

Battle Plans

What are some ways a good man can show kindness to the weak? Is this a sissy thing to do?

How would Jesus describe a real man? How can you be strong and gentle at the same time?

14. Overcoming Your Enemy

YOU CAN OVERCOME AND GROW FROM THE HARD THINGS THAT HAPPEN IN YOUR LIFE.

A Squire Prepares His Heart

Every man faces hard times in his life. Overcoming struggles is what makes a young man into the knight God intends him to be (Romans 5:3-5). In the story, the squire faced a dragon who stole the light of purity from the kingdom. What are some dragons that you have faced? Has someone close to you died? Have you lost a special friend? Have you been tempted to do something wrong? Have you had to make a hard choice or stand up for what was right in a difficult situation?

Facing all these hardships is part of your spiritual training. God will work in your heart as you trust and obey Him, and He will use each trial to develop godly character in your life. Each time the squire made a good choice, he grew closer to his goal. Good choices will help you fulfill your quest too.

The dragon in *The Squire and the Scroll* looked fearsome, but you have an Enemy who is even worse. You must learn how to fight your Enemy, the Devil. He is eager to set up attacks with temptations and wrong thoughts that argue against God's ways of doing things (1 Peter 5:8). But God says you have the authority as a believer to say "No!" to these things because of Jesus who lives in you (James 4:7).

When you are tempted to do wrong or live in fear, tell the Enemy, "In Jesus' name, leave me alone!" Pray for Jesus' blood to protect you from the Devil's attacks (Revelation 12:11a). Jesus is the great Dragon Slayer. He has already defeated the Devil, and He will show you how to overcome all of the Enemy's plans to ruin you.

A Squire's Prayer

Lord, sometimes it's hard to understand that I have an Enemy. I can't see who is trying to destroy me. Show me how to be courageous when I face temptation. Teach me how to say "No!" to wrong choices and thoughts. Make me wise, God, in Your Word, so I can become a mighty knight for You. Make me a dragon slayer! Amen.

Scroll of Truth

"Your enemy the devil prowls around like a roaring lion looking for someone to devour. Resist him, standing firm in the faith."   1 Peter 5:8b-9a

Creative Squire Adventures

Dragon Bowling—Draw a picture of a dragon and make copies of it. Glue the dragons to the fronts of empty soda cans or two-liter bottles. Set them up as a bowling game, using a small ball. Or set them across the top of a fence to knock off with a ball. Remind yourself that you want to practice defeating the Enemy of your soul too!

Target Practice—If your parents agree, work together to make an old-fashioned slingshot. Set up target practice outside, shooting at a two-foot dragon you've drawn on paper or cardboard. Be a wise squire and never use the slingshot for evil purposes, or when not given permission. Make wise choices now; bigger tests await you. Prove that you can be trustworthy like David.

Hero of the Faith: David

David faced some wild animals when he was young. In 1 Samuel 17:34-37, what animals did he face and overcome? How did these experiences prepare him for the battle he was about to face with the giant Goliath? How can this study prepare you to be a dragon slayer?

Battle Plans

What dragons are making your life hard right now? God wants to help you overcome them (read James 1:2-4). How can your parents help?

Are you spending time in God's Word and talking to your heavenly King every day?

15. Finishing Strong

YOU CAN BECOME A MAN OF STRENGTH, INTEGRITY AND EXCELLENCE.

A Squire Prepares His Heart

There may be people in your life who will try to discourage you from your quest. They'll say, "You can't keep yourself pure. You can't make a difference in the world. You can't become anything great. You'll just have to settle for an ordinary life." People may speak the words, but these are all lies from your Enemy. God says that you are already a powerful part of His kingdom if you are following Him with all your mind, heart, soul and strength (Ephesians 1:18-20). Don't let anyone tell you that you can't become a man of greatness!

In pride, the knight told the young boy that he was "only a squire." But the squire came through in the end, didn't he? The squire rescued the lantern and all of the captive men. He became a knight and even a prince! Don't let anyone discourage you by saying you're too young to matter to God. Set an example for people of all ages with your good, godly choices (1 Timothy 4:12).

It's true that we all fail from time to time. When we sin God is faithful to forgive us and clean our hearts (1 John 1:9). So whether you pass a test or fall short in your quest, give every success and failing to God. He will connect all of these experiences to write your life story as a knight—a man after God's own heart (Galatians 6:9).

A Squire's Prayer

Lord, it's so easy to get discouraged. Sometimes I wonder if I can really become the knight You want me to be. Show me how to keep my heart clean and trust that You are making me into a mighty man for Your kingdom. I want to finish strong! Thank You, Lord. Amen.

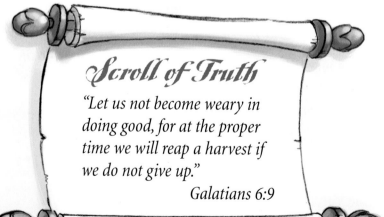

Scroll of Truth

"Let us not become weary in doing good, for at the proper time we will reap a harvest if we do not give up."

Galatians 6:9

Creative Squire Adventures

Reaching the Goal—On a nice day, ask your mom for two placemats that are okay for you to stand on. Go outside your house and stand on one placemat, placing the second placemat right in front of you. Step onto the placemat in front of you, and move the second mat ahead of you again. Continue until you have gone around the house one full time. Was it easy? What was the key to reaching your goal? Read Philippians 3:13b-14 with a parent. How did you just do what the verses said? How can you practice this in your life?

"Can" Drinks—Make your own power drinks. Ask your mom to purchase some canned juices at the store. Read Philippians 4:14 and copy it on labels for each can. Attach the labels with tape or glue. Refrigerate the drinks. Next time you feel discouraged, ask for a "can" drink. The drink will refresh your body as the Bible verse refreshes your spirit!

Hero of the Faith: Peter

Read about Peter in Matthew 14:27-30; Luke 22:54-62; and Acts 4:8-13. God could see who Peter was becoming even when Peter failed terribly. What did Peter do that showed his great faith? How did he fail Jesus? What kind of man did he become as he kept moving toward his goal?

Battle Plans

What did the knight say that might have discouraged the squire? What did the squire do in spite of those words?

How old do you have to be in order to do great things for God?

16. Choosing to Forgive

A GRACIOUS SQUIRE CHOOSES TO FORGIVE THOSE WHO FAIL.

A Squire Prepares His Heart

Have you ever heard of someone who was angry at a person for a long, long time? That's called holding a grudge. When a person refuses to forgive, bitterness and anger fill him up on the inside and begin to poison his life. It's so important that you forgive right away those who hurt you, no matter how many times they do wrong (Matthew 18:21-22).

Pride looks down on those who make mistakes; but sooner or later you will fail too (Proverbs 16:18). Proud men forget that they still sin no matter how well they follow God's path (Romans 3:23; 1 John 1:10).

The squire was not full of selfish pride. Though the knight had failed him terribly, the squire quickly forgave him, as Jesus tells us to (Colossians 3:13). Forgiveness is always a choice. Forgiveness means you release the one who has hurt you, and you allow God to deal with the other person. Revenge is not for you. That is God's business (Romans 12:19).

When you choose to forgive, you free your own heart from the deep pain of the hurt, and you allow God to flood your heart with His peace. Then you can freely show the love of Christ to everyone. You can encourage others to do what's right by loving and forgiving them in spite of their weaknesses (1 Thessalonians 5:14-15).

Avoid the Enemy's trap of bitterness and grudge-holding by forgiving quickly (Ephesians 4:31-32). When you forgive people all through your life, you will be able to keep following the dreams God has given you, and you won't get stuck thinking about the ways you've been hurt.

A Squire's Prayer

Father, sometimes it's hard to remember to forgive someone who has hurt me. I need Your help to train my mind to forgive quickly and to trust in You. Guard my heart and protect me from traps of bitterness, anger and holding grudges. Thank You for the peace that comes when I forgive just as You've forgiven me. Amen.

Scroll of Truth

"Be kind and compassionate to one another, forgiving each other, just as in Christ God forgave you."

Ephesians 4:32

Creative Squire Adventures

Dropping the Weight—Find a heavy weight, like a sack of potatoes or a load of books. Carry it around for half an hour everywhere you go. What a pain! An unforgiving attitude is like that, weighing us down and making life so much harder. It steals our energy and joy; it can even make us sick. What can you do about the burden of an unforgiving heart?

How Many Times?—Ask your mother for some uncooked rice in a bowl. Read Luke 17:3-4. Count out the number of grains of rice that corresponds to the number of times Jesus said to forgive in one day. Now read Matthew 18:21-22. Count out the number of grains of rice that corresponds to the number of times Jesus said to forgive in this passage. Do you think Jesus means for us to keep track and stop forgiving after a certain number of times? Tell your parent what these verses really mean.

Hero of the Faith: Joseph

The amazing scene of forgiveness in Genesis 45:1-15 is an example for us all. What things did Joseph do that made it clear he forgave his brothers? (You may want to read on through verse 28.) What evil did his brothers do to him? Joseph looked for God's plan in his brothers' wickedness. What was it?

Battle Plans

Remember how the squire forgave the knight for letting him down? You can also choose to forgive. Ask God to forgive you; then pray for courage to forgive others and to tell them they are forgiven.

Sometimes living in harmony can be hard. What does 1 Peter 3:8-9a encourage us to do?

41

17. Leading Others on Right Paths

YOU CAN LEAD OTHERS TO GOD BY YOUR EXAMPLE.

A Squire Prepares His Heart

If you're in school you know how the popularity system works. But you weren't meant to think about how much better you are than everyone else. You were created to be a loving leader who would lead others to God through your good example.

The Bible is very clear concerning the subject of favoritism, or treating some people better than others. It's not okay to treat people differently because of their clothes, music choices, skin color, family background, wealth, or anything else (James 2:1-4). Prejudice—wrong judging—is an evil in God's eyes. (See Acts 10:34-35.)

The squire's character made him the kind of man who could lead lost men back to the kingdom. Can you imagine how happy those men must have felt to be set free? The squire was their hero, and he even earned the right to rule over them in the end, all because he had proven himself to be a caring leader.

Don't waste your time spending energy on being cool and fitting into your group. You have so many better things to do! Talk to others about Jesus and how being loving and kind can make their lives better. Lead them out of darkness and into God's light (1 Peter 2:9)!

A Squire's Prayer

God, it's so tempting to try to be popular. Help me believe that I can be something better than cool. Teach me how to be a man of compassion and service. I want to care more about what You think than what anyone else thinks. Free me from the sin of choosing favorites. I want to lead people everywhere to You! Amen.

Scroll of Truth

"If you show favoritism, you sin and are convicted by the law as lawbreakers."

James 2:9

Creative Squire Adventures

Proud or Humble—On a sheet of paper make a column for *Proud People* and a column for *Humble People*. Write what God does for each type of person. (Read Psalm 18:27; 25:9; 31:23; 147:6; Proverbs 3:34; Psalm 149:4; Proverbs 15:26; 16:5; Luke 1:51-52; and James 4:6.)

No Favoritism—Invite a new friend to your house. Choose someone who isn't necessarily popular, or someone you may not have noticed in the past. Enjoy getting to know him, and tell him about the God you believe in, who loves and accepts everyone.

Understanding Prejudice—Check out a book from the library that tells a story about slavery. Take time to understand that prejudice against any group of people breaks God's heart. Talk with your parents about other kinds of prejudice and what you can do to stand against it.

Hero of the Faith: Peter

Peter's vision in Acts 10:9-28 seemed odd at first, but God made it clear that He wanted people to know He shows no favoritism. What miraculous meeting did God set up after Peter's vision? Read verses 34-48 to find the bold things Peter said at this meeting. What happened because of Peter's boldness and willingness to obey God?

Battle Plans

What is your job (1 Peter 2:9)? How can you do this at school and other places?

Is there anything you can do about favoritism or prejudice at school? Discuss this with your parents.

How can popularity be used for good or evil?

43

18. Protecting Ladies' Hearts

A GOOD KNIGHT LEARNS TO PROTECT THE HEARTS OF YOUNG LADIES AROUND HIM.

A Squire Prepares His Heart

Our world is confused about relationships between men and women. Boys and girls should be able to be friends without being teased about being boyfriends and girlfriends. Maybe you've heard people your age talking about *going out* or *dating* when they're not even old enough to drive a car!

Those words are part of a dating game that can break a young person's heart. To you the game may just seem like fun, but to others it can be hurtful (Proverbs 12:18). Breaking up with a girl can make her feel like no one likes her. She may wonder if she is ugly or if something is wrong with her. An unwise girl can make YOU feel that way too.

God never meant for people to play with others' emotions. His plan is that we treat each other with respect and protect each other's feelings, no matter what age we are (1 Timothy 5:1b-2). God wants us to take relationships seriously, not to treat them like a game (1 John 4:7-8). You can honor God and protect girls' hearts by being their friend and watching out for their best interests instead of going out and breaking up with them, one by one.

Now is the time to enjoy group activities with many different friends. Until you are emotionally, physically, spiritually and financially able to provide for a wife, your focus should be on growing in all of these areas and giving all you have to God. If God allows you to marry, your wife will be so glad that you saved your heart just for God and her!

A Squire's Prayer

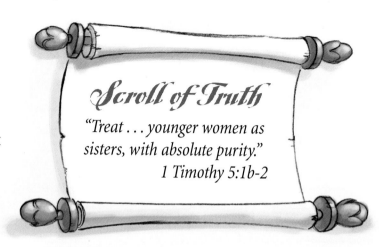

Lord, I am still young, but I can see how important it is to guard my heart and protect the hearts of girls around me. Help me to have healthy friendships with girls and other guys. If You want me to be married some day, I know I can trust You to bring the right girl into my life. Amen.

Scroll of Truth

"Treat . . . younger women as sisters, with absolute purity."
1 Timothy 5:1b-2

Creative Squire Adventures

Knightly Chivalry—Review with your parents how to be courteous to a young lady by opening doors for her, pulling out a chair for her at the table, or carrying something heavy for her. What kind of things would you say . . . or not say? Tonight at dinner, practice with your mom and/or sisters. Ask them to share a time when someone was courteous to them, and how that made them feel.

A Tricky Word—Read 1 Corinthians 13 with your parents and talk about what you read. What does the word *love* mean when God talks about it? What does the world think it means? What do some people your age think it means? How can you show love to others (especially girls) as God wants you to?

Hero of the Faith: Samson

Samson was specially gifted by God, and he was a hero in some ways; but in the matter of relationships with women, he was not wise. Read Judges 14:1-3 and 16:4-21. Samson's parents wanted him to choose a godly wife, but who did he decide to marry? Why was Samson a poor example of purity? How might Samson's story have been different if he had guarded his heart and not played foolish games with Delilah's emotions?

Battle Plans

Why are dating games hurtful?

What words are respectful in describing a girl who is your friend? What words have you heard that are not respectful?

Think of girls who are your friends. How can you help protect their hearts?

If God wants you to marry, your wife is growing up right now. Ask God to protect her heart.

45

19. Enjoying the Rewards of a Pure Heart

IF YOU GUARD YOUR HEART, YOU WILL BE REWARDED IN MANY WAYS.

A Squire Prepares His Heart

There are great rewards in store for those who walk faithfully in their journey with God (Proverbs 11:18). One reward is a good reputation. People will know that you are a hard-working, trustworthy, kind man who will do what's right even when no one is watching (Proverbs 13:6). Just as the squire's obedience brought hope back to the kingdom and filled his king with joy, you will have the privilege of influencing the lives of people around you for the better as you live with integrity for King Jesus.

Another reward is better health. The Bible encourages us to live in obedience to God's laws, avoiding sin, in order to guard our health (Proverbs 3:7-8; 4:20-22). Choose carefully what you eat and what you breathe in. It makes a difference in your health—that's a scientific fact.

If you learn wisdom and live by God's standards, you may receive another reward—a young lady who also serves God. Pure relationships are lasting, true and deep. A marriage is happy when a man and wife know God and are committed to His ways (Proverbs 31:10-12, 23), and a couple that loves God will want to teach their children God's laws.

Whether you marry or not, God will reward you with a purpose-filled adventure. You serve the Creator of the universe who wants more than anything to make you into the knight you were meant to be (Jeremiah 29:11). Nothing can top that! So guard your heart. God's rewards are truly wonderful, and they are well worth any struggles you may face.

A Squire's Prayer

Lord, I don't want to miss a single reward, so I will guard my heart carefully. If I marry I want to be a husband who will bless his wife and children. More than anything else I want to enjoy this journey with You and become a knight who brings You praise. I will serve You patiently and trust You for good rewards in Your timing. Amen.

Scroll of Truth

"He who sows righteousness reaps a sure reward."
Proverbs 11:18b

Creative Squire Adventures

The Rewards of Obedience—For one day let your parents catch you in the act of obedience and reward you! Agree on some amount of reward money (an age-appropriate amount) per obedient act. We obey God in response to His love for us. Can you think of a way to use your reward money to show your love for Him?

The Perfect Princess—The squire's reward included the king's daughter! Her character made her a great prize. Trace your mother's hand (or the hand of a woman in your family) on paper. Read Proverbs 31:10-31; inside the hand write the qualities in the life of a "wife of noble character." Ask God to keep His hand of protection on your wife, if you are to marry some day.

Hero of the Faith: Joseph

Joseph was a man of integrity; he was chosen to raise Jesus and to be His dad on earth. Read about him in Matthew 1:18-25. God asked some difficult things of Joseph, and Joseph obeyed in spite of what people might have thought. What were these difficult things? Why were they hard? What kind of wife do you think Mary was? (See Luke 1:28, 30.) Was Joseph rewarded?

Battle Plans

Is it enough to obey only part of a command?

If you obey but grumble the whole time, is this obedience from the heart?

When are some times that you are likely to disobey? Pray with your parents about these struggles.

20. Building a Generation of Knights

YOU CAN HELP BUILD A NEW GENERATION OF MEN WHO ARE COMMITTED TO PURITY AND INTEGRITY.

A Squire Prepares His Heart

There aren't a lot of unselfish men of integrity in the world. Many men are self-centered and do whatever it takes to get ahead, no matter who it hurts. You've probably met some young men like this at school, who only look out for themselves and what's good for them. (See 2 Timothy 3:1-5.)

What if young men found out that there is a better way? What if they started serving others, respecting girls, guarding their hearts, honoring parents and teachers, and reaching out to those in need? The world would be such a different place! (See Psalm 1:1-3.)

The Squire and the Scroll and this study guide were written with the hope that young men like you would find the courage to become men of integrity and help change the world. If you choose to take this challenge, you will guard your five senses, enter marriage with a pure heart and body, and someday teach your own children to love and serve God (Psalm 112:2).

There are three things you need to do. First, decide to live your life God's way. Second, pray for friends who love Jesus so you can stand firm together and encourage each other to live godly lives (Ecclesiastes 4:9-12; Proverbs 27:17). Third, look for opportunities to share God's ways with people who don't know His truth.

Jesus can use you and your Christian friends to show others how to stand for what is right. Ask God to teach you how to do these things. You are part of a new generation that can bring spiritual life and light back to our nation and even to the world!

A Squire's Prayer

God, thank You for choosing me to be a part of this new generation. I'm honored that You have an important job for me to do. I'm just one person, but I know that I can do great things with Your strength. Help me to make friends with other Christians and to bravely reach out to those who don't know You yet. Amen.

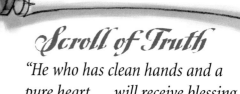

Scroll of Truth

"He who has clean hands and a pure heart . . . will receive blessing from the LORD. . . . Such is the generation of those who seek him."
Psalm 24:4-6b

Creative Squire Adventures

Calling All Disciples—Ask your parents if you may invite some good friends over for a campout. Choose young men you think would want to do things God's way. That night around a campfire, read stories about Jesus and the disciples. Talk about making an agreement to be courageous men like the disciples.

Not Easily Broken—Find six to ten twigs from a tree outside. Can you break one? Two? How many twigs can you break at the same time? In the same way, men can stand strong when they work together and support each other as friends. How many "twigs" do you have in your group of friends? Read Ecclesiastes 4:9-12 for another example.

Hero of the Faith: Jesus

Jesus gave us a great model for teaching others in Mark 3:13-19. What did He do? What does Acts 4:13 say about some of these men? Why do you think Jesus chose the men He did?

Battle Plans

Why is it important to have strong, godly friends?

Why should you share what you know about the Christian life with others? Talk with your parents about the Great Commission (found in Matthew 28:19-20).

21. Passing On a Legacy

A DEVOTED KNIGHT PREPARES HIS OWN CHILDREN TO SERVE AND HONOR GOD WITH PURE HEARTS.

A Squire Prepares His Heart

If one or both of your parents are going through this book with you, then you know they are committed to leaving a legacy. That means they are preparing you to live an amazing, godly life, not just in their home but in your home later, and long after your parents have gone to be with Jesus.

A godly wife is a gift from the Lord (Proverbs 18:22; 19:14), and so are children (Psalm 127:3). Parents have the privilege of showing and telling their children about God's love for them. Their words and example will help protect their children from falling into the sin and misery that many young people who don't know God will experience (Proverbs 3:1-2).

If you have a family of your own some day, you will be able to teach your children what your parents are teaching you now—how to follow God, be people of integrity and purity, and pass the same gift on to their own children (Psalm 145:4-5). Just as the squire taught his son from the scroll, you will be able to teach your children the Word of God, and they will be able to teach theirs (Psalm 22:30-31). This is a godly heritage that protects a family line and provides God with people who serve Him and His purposes on earth for many years to come.

If God does not call you to raise a family, you will be able to devote all your energy to serving God in a special way. Married or unmarried, God's knights are His ambassadors. They leave a legacy of His love with everyone they meet.

A Squire's Prayer

Lord, I want to leave a legacy of love with everyone I meet. If a wife and family are in my future, I know You will show me that in Your perfect time. No matter what adventures are ahead, I want people to think of You when they think of my life. My goal is to honor Your name. Amen.

Scroll of Truth

"No weapon forged against you will prevail, and you will refute every tongue that accuses you. This is the heritage of the servants of the LORD...."   Isaiah 54:17

Creative Squire Adventures

A Family Legacy—Look at some family photos of relatives who have died. Let your parents tell you about your relatives and about the traits they've passed on to you. Were they Christians? Did they work hard? Did they manage money well? How did their choices benefit you? Now look at a photograph or make a drawing of yourself. Write on the back what you would like others to say about you many years from now. Keep the photo where you can read it often to remind yourself that you are leaving a legacy every day.

Heroes of the Faith: Elijah and Elisha

Read 1 Kings 19:16, 19-21 and 2 Kings 2:6-14. An important legacy was passed to Elisha when Elijah threw his coat over Elisha's shoulders. What was this legacy that made it possible for Elisha to part the water? How is the relationship of these two men like the one between a father and son?

Battle Plans

How can you leave a legacy even if you don't raise a family some day?

What legacy is your favorite hero leaving in the world?

Why is it important to include purity in your family legacy?

Parents' Compass
Introduction

The Parents' Compass material is a tool for you to use to set your son's feet on the right path toward purity and godly manhood. This section of the book is designed to give you additional talking points as you get into the life of your son and provide opportunities to expand on the lessons or tackle tougher issues. The numbered Compass Tips on the following pages correspond to the Life Lessons throughout the devotional. God gives parents and authorities in children's lives the responsibility of leadership—living a worthy example and training them in God's ways. Be sure that you are walking in these paths and modeling purity for your son.

Begin with positive affirmation. Let your son know how important he is to you, and tell him your desires for him as he prepares to enter manhood like the young squire. Also, reassure him that during this study it's okay to ask ANY QUESTIONS he might have, even if they seem embarrassing.

Dads (or mentors), God gives you the mandate to help your son develop a secure sense of his own manhood. You are the primary communicator of the principles which follow. Every boy desperately needs and yearns to be loved, accepted, affirmed and mentored by his father (and other men). In a culture that glorifies impurity, <u>he needs you to teach him the truth</u>, even if he acts like he doesn't want it. If you are filling the role of a mentor, don't discount your valuable influence.

It is also important for him to identify with the men around him, to grow up feeling like he is one of the guys. Involve him in everyday activities around the house, in the yard, working on the car, assisting with meals, etc. Keep in mind that you are not only teaching your son skills; more importantly you are teaching him a way of interacting with men, showing him how men think and process, how to treat women, and how to respond to life with a masculine mindset. Be careful, especially if he is sensitive, not to put him down or belittle his abilities. Praise him often. Encourage right actions. Give him physical affection. When he fails don't let him sink into self-pity or defeat, but encourage him with love and praise.

Moms (or caregivers), by the time a boy is ten he should begin the normal process of identifying himself with the men around him. You can help by viewing him that way more and more as he grows, assigning him small things that "only men can do," and reinforcing steps that lead him to develop and appreciate his masculinity. It is important not to shield your son when Dad wants to be rough-and-tumble with him or make him work. Be careful not to put men down—your son is paying close attention to your attitude toward men. You want him to identify with men, not distance himself because of negative comments.

Your son can become a valiant knight, a champion for Jesus Christ and the kingdom of God. As you share in the adventure of his spiritual development, you will have the exciting blessing of cooperating with God's Spirit in reaching your son's heart.

1. Becoming God's Pure Knight

Take some time during this lesson to briefly recount the stories of Daniel and his three friends, Shadrach, Meshach and Abednego. These are true heroes! Help your child think of people he knows (including family members) who have exemplified heroic behavior. (This can also include heroes from the past or modern-day movie characters, if they measure up morally.) Next, help your child to remember times when he has behaved heroically by helping, being obedient, or standing up for his faith. Pointing out these small victories will encourage him. Be careful not to belittle your son if he feels timid right now. Speak as though he is growing strong—show him how God is working in his life—and he will eventually rise to the challenges before him!

2. Choosing to Serve the King

If your son has not received Christ, take time to clearly explain how to make this important decision. Explain that surrender to Christ includes giving up what he wants in order to pursue what God wants. Explain how Jesus will empower him to live victoriously. Discuss the reward of heaven. Talk about Christ's example in laying down His life for us and about our service for Him. If you find it helpful, use the *Romans Road* (Romans 3:23; 6:23; 5:8; 10:9-10, 13) to present the salvation message. It is a special privilege to lead your child to Christ. Be sensitive and patient, especially if your son says he is not quite ready to make this decision. Allow God's Spirit to continue working in his heart, drawing your son into the Word of truth (John 16:13).

3. Reaching Dreams God Has Given You

Discuss the dreams God has given to you. Talk about times when you did or didn't attempt to accomplish those dreams God's way, and what resulted. Talk about some of the dreams your son might have. Be supportive. How can your son approach these dreams God's way? Help him to bring one of those dreams into simple, initial reality, beginning with the *Reaching for the Goal* activity mentioned in this lesson.

4. Protecting Your Purity

To illustrate the concept of guarding the heart, compare it to eating habits, like this: "To keep your body healthy you must eat healthy foods. To keep your spirit healthy you must take in good spiritual food. Impure junk that you take in through your eyes and ears will make your spirit sick, just as junk food will make your body sick." Be sure your son understands that rewards of purity (joy, peace and freedom) come from a clear conscience toward God and others. In an age-appropriate way, if your son is ready, discuss the importance of saving himself for his wedding day, and emphasize that purity is important both in marriage and throughout all of life.

5. Accepting the Protection of Authority

This lesson is not an opportunity to tell your son, "See? You need to obey me!" It's so easy to focus on rules instead of relationship. Respect and listen to each other. Teach your son that honoring and obeying parents is a foundation for honoring and obeying God. Emphasize your desire to protect him as he becomes a man of character, making life choices that he will never regret (Proverbs 23:26). If you have personal memories of how obedience and respect (or a lack of obedience and respect) affected your own life, prayerfully consider

sharing them. Your son will learn much from your transparent example and honest expressions of regret. Let him know how pleased you are that he is eager to obey the Lord. Pray for your son, asking for God's protection over his life choices. NOTE: Mentors and those who disciple young boys must be careful to preserve honor for the parent while teaching and modeling a godly example.

6. Living by the Scroll

Our lives are very full and busy, but setting aside time with your son is worth the cost, especially when you consider the payoffs in his life! Make whatever sacrifices are necessary to discuss the lessons together. Find creative ways to memorize Bible verses. Play worship songs that are based on Scripture. Find Bible stories in contemporary language with pictures, and teach your son to love reading. And since your son is absorbing so much from your example, pray constantly for a greater love for the Word in your own life. You will both be amazed at the good fruit that comes as you devote yourselves to God's Word!

7. Guarding Your Ears

Talking about music choices can be a touchy subject. Be open, and answer your son's questions. Be clear about lyrics that are unacceptable. In the *All Ears* exercise in this lesson, take stock of your own entertainment choices too. Discuss how secular lyrics are planted in our hearts, but also how music can be a powerful tool to memorize Scripture. Discuss the meaning of *filthy talk* and what that includes. Read Proverbs 20:5. Strive to discern the matters of your child's heart, and come alongside to help him understand how to respond to any negative voices in the culture, or even from you. Let your son remember your blessings, your positive instructions, and God's wonderful truths.

8. Guarding Your Eyes

Our society is very dangerous to your son because of what he may see. Be fearless as you discuss the topic of pornography at a level he can understand. Train him to understand the dangers of the Internet, and (at an age-appropriate level) what makes a magazine unfit. As he nears puberty discuss the changes that will come in his feelings about girls, and prepare him for pure relationships. Dad, help your son understand that eye temptations are every man's battle—that he is not unique in his struggles. Explain that when a guy looks at images of nude women, a chemical hormone (*epinephrine*) is released into the pleasure center of his brain, and the desire to view more of these images becomes addictive. If he wants to avoid this addiction, he must be careful to guard his eyes. Teach him how to yield his eyes to God's control. Don't let Satan's lie of "boys will be boys" keep you from preparing your son for this crucial battle. (If *you* are struggling in this area, seek God and wise counsel for the strength and resources to conquer your own sin habits.)

9. Choosing Friends Wisely

Take some time during this lesson to talk about the friends your son has and how they affect him. Be as specific as possible, but be gentle in questioning loyalties. Use personal examples from your life or of those near to you that model how a good or bad example can affect a friend or friendship. Sometimes a child has few others to choose from for companionship. If your child is struggling with this (especially in the junior high years), become a faithful prayer partner and pray for a friend to come into his life who will be an encouragement.

10. Guarding Your Mouth

Foul language is like a disease that catches and spreads. Coarse talk or disrespectful tones of voice don't have to be a part of any family's life. Your example is what your son will follow. Do your best to be a positive example to him so he can be strong if he comes into contact with boys who don't use their tongues with integrity. If you have failed in the past, be honest and state your intent to do better. We're all growing, and your son will appreciate your honesty.

If a young man can understand and control his desire to satisfy his taste buds in contrast to meeting his body's basic need for nutrition, he will also be able to clearly understand how to control his sexual appetites as he matures. Mom, you can help your son by preparing nutritionally balanced meals and by watching that what he eats in large quantities is actually healthy.

11. Guarding Your Hands and Feet

Explain that wisdom for the paths of life is found in God's Word. But talking about paths can also tie into choices about touch—issues of purity. Define *personal touch* and help him understand what kind of touch is appropriate with young women. At the appropriate age and readiness, bravely define clear boundaries for him (or his buddies in the locker room will), and discuss the matters of sexual dreams and self-stimulation. Your son may be crippled by guilt if he doesn't understand these issues, so seek God's guidance and explain gently. Define healthy touch and explain that anything outside that realm is questionable in his singleness. And don't forget to explain that touch in marriage is exceptional, beautiful and blessed.

12. Serving the King with Every Breath

This lesson is a wonderful opportunity to do two things. First, on a practical level, discuss the dangers of cigarettes and other potential poisons (drugs, alcohol, inhalants) that can destroy breathing and health in general. Share stories you know of those who have suffered because of these addictive substances. If there is a family example, be discreet and show compassion for the struggling relative, but discuss the tragedy of lost opportunities as well as God's restoring grace. Then, on a spiritual level, talk about what God wants breath to be used for—praising and glorifying Him. Remind your son to ask to be filled with the Holy Spirit daily so he is empowered to understand God's Word and to live it. Remind him that he will some day stand before God, and it is important to trust and obey God now.

13. Reaching Out to the Weak

In this lesson focus on the blessings mentioned in Psalm 41 as a reward for kindness toward the weak (see *Rescuing the Weak* activity). Emphasize what manliness looks like through God's eyes. Steer your son clear of the tough-guy image, and pair gentleness with strength, courage with servanthood. Share examples of family members, neighbors, or friends at school who are sick, troubled, or picked on. If there is a good male servant example in your family, talk about some of their good deeds and how others respect that person.

14. Overcoming Your Enemy

Share your own testimony regarding traps the Enemy set for you, especially when you were a teenager. How did you overcome? How did you respond when you failed and when God forgave you? How did those experiences shape you? Share wisely and specifically,

in an age-appropriate manner, but be courageous. If your son is interested in girls, review how to guard his eyes from immodest, flirtatious young women and the indecent images around him. Explain how these traps from Satan lead to specific sin. Contrast this with the rewards of a pure heart. If your son is in a season of hardship (loss of a friend or loved one, difficult family issues, etc.), encourage him to bravely press on.

15. Finishing Strong

Many young men become discouraged along the path to becoming God's man. A harsh word or difficult circumstance can make them wonder if it's worth the struggle. You can answer with a definite, "Yes, it is!" Let your son know that you believe he's capable of ministry now, not just when he grows up. Psalm 139 will remind your son how much God values him. Allow him to pray, serve and minister as God makes opportunities available. If he fails he will need your comfort and strength. Teach him how to handle failures. Give him no doubt that you will still love him when he makes mistakes. Help him pursue the goal to be like Jesus.

16. Choosing to Forgive

Talk about the heavy weight that an unforgiving attitude puts on a young man's heart. Many men suffer from anger and even the physical disabilities of high blood pressure and stress because of past wrongs that are not forgiven. Encourage your son to drop this heavy load. Share personal experiences of forgiveness and lack of forgiveness, and how each affected you. If wrong has been done to your son recently, pray with him and walk him through the process of forgiveness. Explain Jesus' call to forgive others as an ongoing process. Examine your own heart. Do you need to humble yourself and ask your son's forgiveness for ways you may have failed or disappointed him?

17. Leading Others on Right Paths

If your son is a member of the "popular" crowd, emphasize his responsibility to use his social position as a tool to help and encourage others to be their best. If he doesn't fit in well, focus on the refreshing news that popularity is not what God requires of him. God has a much better plan! In either case, major on the call to lead others out of darkness and into God's light (1 Peter 2:9). Encourage your son to be a positive example, not hurtful or showing prejudice. Explain that when he graduates from school popularity won't count as much as being a respected, good, kind man.

18. Protecting Ladies' Hearts

Our children are playing dating games earlier and earlier, and they are breaking each others' hearts. This kind of activity may seem harmless but it does not build a solid, courageous foundation for relationships as our boys near manhood. In fact, breaking up is a great practice run for divorce. If your son is younger and not yet interested in girls, common courtesy in speech and action are sufficient to teach and model; but if he's older and showing interest, decisively address issues of sexuality and purity. Explain that it's not just in the matter of intercourse, but through touch and emotional teasing that young people follow dangerous, hurtful and ungodly paths. Provide accurate, age-appropriate information. Guard him from wrong information and attitudes that could come from others.

19. Enjoying the Rewards of a Pure Heart

This lesson gives you an opportunity to talk with your son about the rewards of obedience. Share personal stories of good choices you've made in obedience to God and how God rewarded you; or discuss the rewards of others who did things God's way, even when it was hard. This is also a perfect lesson to talk about the beauty of a God-centered marriage. Tell your son openly what you love about your spouse (or the qualities that you would value if such a person were present). Express your own regrets and how you want life to be different for him. Your passionate, honest communication is what counts.

20. Building a Generation of Knights

Take time to discuss ways that your son might develop friendships with other young believers. Encourage him to find buddies with similar goals: (1) becoming strong to avoid sin, and (2) becoming a positive, godly influence on this hurting generation. Be creative. Consider and discuss starting a regular gathering for a few boys in your home once or twice each month. You could include a short Bible study, an act of service, or a time of prayer for those in need. How does your son respond as you suggest these ideas? Pray that he will be an example to others as he learns from your example. This is discipleship!

21. Passing On a Legacy

It's difficult for any child to picture their future. Your son needs to know from you what a joy it is to grow up, marry and have children. Share how you love the family you're a part of and how they have changed your life. Include memories of your wedding and childbirth. (If a divorce took place, don't be afraid to honestly share how you wish things could have happened differently.) Share what you hope your son will gain from these lessons and other "God information" you have given him. Also share a story of someone who is single but serving God with joy. Impress on your son the fact that he will always be influencing other lives—it will be up to him to decide *how* he influences them.

Squires of the Lantern Ceremony Guide

The **Squires of the Lantern Ceremony** is a wonderful opportunity for you as a parent to inspire your young squire to pursue integrity and purity as he enters adolescence. The ceremony can be planned for a private or group setting. Although a private setting is special, *we encourage a small, intimate group setting* that will allow the boys to interact and gain accountability. This memorable, bonding event will offer encouragement for young boys as they grow up together.

The following are only suggestions. Feel free to add personal creativity as you discern your child's heart and level of maturity. We would love to hear from you if you have any additional ideas. Write to **Ideas@ReviveOurHearts.com**.

Suggested Age for Groups

We suggest that a group consist of 3rd – 6th-grade boys who have gone through at least half of the Life Lessons devotional guide. This mix of ages will allow the older boys to set examples and help the younger squires-in-training.

The Private Ceremony

Consider planning a camping getaway weekend with your son, or plan an intimate setting in your home or back yard. The private setting gives an opportunity for a more serious atmosphere similar to the blessing ceremony found in Genesis 27:25-29 for the firstborn son. Fathers (or both parents) and sons may participate, perhaps with grandparents and family members looking on. Single moms, you may want to ask a godly male mentor to participate in this rite of passage for your son and to offer a spoken or written tribute in addition to yours.

The Group Ceremony

Whether you choose to plan this in a home, back yard, church, gym, or open field, be creative in making this a special ceremony. It is best to limit your ceremony to no more than twelve boys. It will take at least five minutes for each father (parent) to carry out his tribute to his son. These are holy and bonding moments for everyone and should not be rushed. It is best to set the ceremony date far enough out so that parents and sons will complete at least half of their workbook before the ceremony.

If most of your young men and boys are comfortable with wearing costumes, dads and sons may want to dress up in royal attire as kings, knights, squires, or soldiers for the ceremony. Be sensitive to the men involved and do what seems to work best for your group.

Planning the Ceremony

- Set the special date/time/place for the ceremony.
- Call or meet with parents who have completed most of the Life Lessons. Give a brief explanation of the heart and purpose behind the Squires of the Lantern Ceremony and the importance of boys having a rite of passage as they are entering their adolescent years. Give a brief description of the order and plan of the ceremony.
- Share the importance of the parents' personal involvement in giving a blessing for their sons. Refer hesitant parents to the example given on page 64. Encourage them to put something similar into their own words, and remind them that no blessing will be inadequate if it is shared from the heart.
- Share the cost of the gift presentation with the parents. Have order forms available and samples on hand for observation. Order gifts at least four weeks ahead of time.
- Boys can come dressed as a squire or knight if your group is comfortable with this. You might consider preparing ahead of time and providing a simple tunic like the Knights of the Lantern wore in the story. Tunics slip over the head and could be tied with a cord (see next-to-last page in the storybook).
- Purchase or borrow a real sword to use during the ceremony.
- Plan refreshments or a special meal. In keeping with the medieval theme, you might consider serving turkey drumsticks, or cookies shaped like crests, crowns, or swords. Secure servers—perhaps the moms.
- Secure a photographer who is not involved with the ceremony. You will want to capture these priceless moments!
- You will need four designated men to pose as Greeter, Ceremony Host, King, and First Knight. Encourage these men to dress in royal attire if possible. The King and the Ceremony Host will need proper preparation on their speaking parts. Sample speaking parts are given that may be rewritten as needed (see Suggested Order of Ceremony).
- Purchase or spray-paint a cardboard box to make a treasure chest. It should be big enough to hold the gifts and royal certificates for the presentation.
- Download or purchase the official commemoration Squire Certificate for each boy at **www.ReviveOurHearts.com/squire**.
- Plan décor for the area where the presentation will take place (see Royal Décor below).

Royal Décor

Decorations can be as simple or elaborate as you like. (Moms will be great at this!) Be creative, but if you need some help use the picture in the book of the king knighting the faithful squire—a castle theme background. Decorations might include a knight's armor, shields, swords and medieval artifacts. Set up a table for refreshments. Choose regal colors and accent the table with a lantern. If you choose to conduct your ceremony outside, you may use lanterns, torches, or a campfire. (Always use caution with open fire and curious young boys.)

Set up two thrones. One simple throne is for the father to sit on while blessing his son. The second empty throne represents Christ as our true King. Simply place shiny material over these chairs. For King Jesus' chair, place a crown on the empty seat. Display a lantern near the throne to represent the Lantern of Purest Light. (You may purchase battery-operated lanterns if you like.) Place the special gifts and royal certificates for the boys' presentation inside the treasure chest nearby, along with the sword for the ceremony. Expand on these ideas and have fun!

Suggested Order of Ceremony

- **Greeter:** Dressed in costume, the Greeter may want to welcome each boy as Squire _____ (name) and dads as Sir _____ (name) and direct them to the refreshments. If you are serving a meal, have everyone wait for a welcome and prayer. Plan 15 minutes for refreshments, 30 minutes for meal. You may want to provide nametags for the knights (dads) and squires.
- **Royal Squire Tunics (Optional):** If you provide the boys with royal squire tunics like those in the book, distribute them to the boys as they enter.
- **Ceremony Host:** Welcome everyone and give a short explanation about this special event. Lead guests from the refreshments to the ceremony area. (Encourage the boys to take a restroom break before the ceremony begins.)
- Have parents and sons sit together (or sons on the floor) just prior to the ceremony.

Ceremony Host: *Royal families of the realm, we are gathered here to honor our young squires for diligently working through the* Life Lessons from the Squire and the Scroll *and to officially induct them as Squires of the Lantern.*

Young men, tonight this ceremony symbolizes that you are entering a new quest in your life. Just before the squire left home to pursue his dream of knighthood, his parents presented him with two gifts. Does anyone remember what they were? (Wait for responses.)

> *1) He received a scroll to guide him through life.*
> *2) He received a special blessing and charge from his parents. Your parents will have that same opportunity tonight.*

There was something else the squire received as well. That was a promise—a promise of reward from God in return for faithfully guarding his heart. Our God and King (point to King Jesus' throne) is present with us tonight. He has granted to each of us that same promise of reward if we too will faithfully guard our hearts. Young men, we are so proud of you. You are standing on the threshold of entering manhood. To celebrate this special time we have prepared a ceremony in your honor.

Host (Prayer): *King Jesus, we honor You and thank You for Your presence with us. Bless this ceremony, these families, and these sons as we honor them tonight. Let all that is done in this ceremony glorify You as we seek to commit ourselves to integrity and purity. Amen.*

- **Optional:** Choose five boys to recite one of the five truths from the scroll in the story and read a verse that goes with each one.
- **Optional:** Ask two boys to briefly share their favorite scene from the story of the squire. Ask what special lesson they might have learned from going through this study with their parents.

Ceremony Host: *We have someone who wants to share his favorite part of the story to help prepare us for what is ahead. Welcome King _____.*

King (sits on throne and reads the **last five pages** of the story of *The Squire and the Scroll*; gives a brief affirmation to all the dads and boys for completing this initial quest; ends with these words): *We have just read that the king founded the Knights of the Lantern. You are now beginning your journey toward that knighthood by becoming squires. Gentlemen, because of your dedication to the words of the Scroll and to the defense of the Lantern of Purity, and because of your desire to serve our King Jesus—on His behalf, I now institute a new order* *of protectors: the Squires of the Lantern!*

King (Charge to the Fathers): *Fathers, please stand. Your son's journey and quest for manhood has begun. Do you, therefore, dedicate yourself to the continued support and training of your son in the three goals of the Squires of the Lantern: to live by the Scroll (the Word of God), to serve the Eternal King (Jesus), and to train your son to be a man of integrity by defending and protecting the Lantern of Purity? If so, answer, "I do."*

King (Charge to the Sons): *Young men, please stand in front of your fathers, but facing me. Fathers, please place your hands on your sons' shoulders. This is a very serious moment, young men, and I want you to listen carefully. We are all so pleased by how you have faithfully run the race that is set before you. You are about to embark on the next part of your journey toward manhood as you enter your teen years. This will require a greater amount of courage, integrity and faithfulness to your Eternal King. It will not always be an easy journey. At times you will be tempted to go your own way, give in to temptations, or give up in the midst of difficult challenges.*

The person standing behind you believes in you and is there to continue to give you guidance. This person stands confident in God's grace, which will sustain you to the very end of your life, that you might one day hear your King say, "Well done, good and faithful servant." Today you are about to step forward into a new world, a world full of choices, opportunities, challenges and dangers. However, the world can also be full of blessings and rewards as your King has promised, if you are willing to faithfully guard your heart and follow His precepts and principles found in His Word. The theme verse for our study was, "How can a young man keep his way pure? By living according to God's Word" (Psalm 119:29). This truth is something only you can choose to believe and embrace in your heart as a lifestyle.

Now, young men, I must ask you a serious question. Is it the desire of your heart (as it was for the squire in the book) to continue to dedicate yourselves to: 1) Living by the Scroll (Word of God), 2) Serving your Eternal King, and 3) Defending and protecting the Lantern of Purity for yourself and others? To the best of your ability, if this is your desire, respond by answering, "It is."

King (calling for his First Knight): *Bring the king's sword.*

First Knight: Presents sword, kneeling before the king.

King (takes the sword, holding it up high): *Let the blessing ceremony begin.* (The king rises and, with sword in hand, steps to the left of the throne.)

King's First Knight (stands by the king's throne on the right side where the treasure chest is, and calls the first dad forward): *I call Sir _____.* (The first dad will come and bow his head before the king. The rest are seated.)

King: *To whom do you wish to give tribute?*

Father: *My son, Squire _____.* (Be sure fathers are informed of this duty ahead of time. Father takes throne. Son is summoned

and asked to kneel at father's feet.)

Father: Shares his blessing for his squire (see sample blessing given on page 64). We encourage you to have the freedom to put this into your own words and to add personal information regarding your own son. Share from your heart.

After the father gives his blessing (should be no longer than five minutes), he stands, takes the sword from the king, and delivers the following lines while tapping his son on each shoulder with the flat side of the blade: *I, Sir _____ (father's full name), as your father, mentor and friend, do hereby welcome you, my son _____ (son's full name), into the order of the Squires of the Lantern.* (Father hands sword back to the king.)

   • **Father's Prayer:** (Father kneels with son, prays over him, then embraces him. Father and son rise and face the king.)

King (to all boys): *Young men, the king promised great honor and reward to the one who completed the quest to return the Lantern. On this day your father would like to present each of you with a gift to commemorate this special occasion.* (Brief explanation of gift, see page 65.) *First, this gift is to honor you and let you know that your father (parents) is (are) standing with you. Second, it is to serve as a reminder to you that great rewards await those who choose to live by the goals of the Squires of the Lantern.* (This will only need to be said once for the first squire. For the other boys, the king may simply say to the father, *Do you have a presentation?*)

First Knight: Takes gift and squire certificate from treasure chest and hands to father.

Father: *Son, will you receive this gift as a reminder of your calling as a squire and as a symbol of love and prayers from my heart to yours?* (Father may wish to embrace his son here. Father and son are then seated.)

First Knight: Calls for second father, etc. Provide list of names. (<u>NOTE</u>: It may be helpful to rehearse the first father's presentation prior to the ceremony so the others will easily follow.)

Ceremony Host (after completion of entire ceremony): *Squires, this ceremony does not make you a man, but symbolizes that you are stepping into the journey of manhood. The choices you make from this moment on will determine the man you will become and whom you will serve. Let me remind you again that great honor and reward await those who faithfully guard their hearts. And how does a young man keep his heart pure? By living according to God's Word. Your goal must be to dedicate your entire life to this task. Choose wisely, young squires. Remember, some day in the future you may be standing here with your own son.*

King: *Now let us give honor and blessing to our King of Kings. As a symbol of our love, let us all face the True King's chair and give honor to Him by bowing and giving thanks and a final blessing and prayer of dedication over all the fathers and sons.* (You might consider giving a time of silence first for everyone to respond privately before their King—then end with a public prayer.)

   • Take pictures of dads sitting on the throne with their sons standing beside them.

The Blessing

The opportunity to bless your son in the following way can prove to be a special bonding and holy moment—a memory that will last a lifetime. Let your words flow from your heart. Do not let the crowd intimidate you. No words from you will be inadequate. Provided below is a simple guide to help you, but we encourage you to personalize these next statements and put them into your own words. As your son is kneeling before you, look into his eyes and be *fearlessly tender*. The <u>spoken word</u> and <u>meaningful touch</u> were two of the main components of the blessing ceremony in Genesis 27:25-29. So put your hand on his shoulder, knee, or hand and look into his eyes as you talk to him. Block out everyone else who is present—focus on your son.

Helpful hints to incorporate into your blessing

- Keep it to five minutes or less; make it personal and share from your heart.
- Share the joy and feelings you had when your son was placed into your care, and the joy of watching him grow into a young man.
- Mention special memories you've shared together or the things you have watched him accomplish.
- Include how you are pleased to see special character qualities in his life, or a virtue that you see developing in his heart. Share a verse, perhaps, that speaks of this quality.
- Affirm your unconditional love for your son and your desire to stand beside him as he becomes a man.
- Express your hopes for courage, purity, integrity, etc., as he walks through his teen years.
- Pray with a sincere heart of faith over your son. Include your continued dedication to mentor and support him. Guard your own heart from placing too high an expectation on your son. This is not to become a law to the child, but rather a prayer of blessing, tribute and dedication to the Lord.
- Give meaningful hugs.

Sample Blessing

___[Son's Full Name]___, my son and courageous squire: The first time I held you in my arms, an overwhelming sense of joy and responsibility swept over me that I cannot explain. I want you to know that I love you very much. I've so enjoyed watching you grow up—filling your pockets with creepy critters, playing baseball, and hitting your first home run. We've done a lot of guy things together and made wonderful memories. I am thankful for your servant-leadership, and so pleased that you see yourself as the protector and man of the home, looking out for your mom and little sister when I am not there. I know you will make a great husband and dad some day.

Son, I see so many wonderful character qualities in you that I know God is going to develop and continue to mature in your heart. I see your self-discipline and perseverance on the ball field. I see your loyal friendship. God says in Hosea 6:6a that He delights in loyalty rather than sacrifice. Let me remind you to continue to make wise friends who will build you up and not pull you down. Follow those who follow the Lord. Most of all I see your desire to know and please your Heavenly King. That is so important! May your love for Him and His Word continue to grow even stronger.

Time has passed so quickly, and now you are standing on the threshold of manhood, ready to take on the challenges of the world, ready to seek and fulfill the purposes for which God has created you. God has a unique and special plan for your life. In Jeremiah 29:11 God says He knows the thoughts that He thinks toward you, thoughts of peace and not of evil, to give you a future and a hope. Part of that plan is that you become the godly man He intends for you to be. Some of the challenges you will face will not be easy. It will take great courage to choose to do what is right. At times you may falter and fail—all men do at times. Learn from your failures and victories and let them make you stronger. Whether you are standing or have fallen, I will always be here for you, ready to extend a hand and heart of support.

Like the young squire in the book, guard your heart and keep it pure at all costs. Choose wisely, with every challenge or test, to do what is right, filtering everything through the Word of God. Son, I want God to bless you abundantly and cause His face to shine on you so that His purest light and love can shine brightly to others in the darkness. May He raise you up to be a leader of men who gallantly and courageously leads others to our Eternal King. God bless you, my son.

Visit **www.ReviveOurHearts.com/squire** for more information and to print out the squire certificate. Or you can order from:

Revive Our Hearts
P.O. Box 2000
Niles, MI 49120
1-800-569-5959

Send your creative ideas and comments to **Ideas@ReviveOurHearts.com**.

Gift for the Squires of the Lantern Ceremony

The Shield and Lantern Watch is a special, memorable gift to present to your son during the ceremony commemorating his journey towards manhood. As your squire wears this special watch, the different symbols (shield, cross, sword, lantern, and scroll) will remind him of key life lessons on his daily quest.

This one-of-a-kind watch will also be a wonderful reminder of your love, support and prayers every time your son wears it. It is made to hang from a belt loop and is uniquely shaped in the form of a shield that opens to reveal the time. Each time he lifts the shield cover to see the time, Psalm 119:9 will remind him to guard his heart and to withstand temptation as he learns to serve the King.

Presentation of the Gift

When you present your squire with this watch, explain the meaning of each symbol and discuss the theme verse. Here are some thoughts to help.

- **The Shield:** The shield is a picture of God's protection. He has promised not to let you be tempted more than you can bear. He gave you the shield of faith to guard you from the Enemy's lies and attacks.
- **The Cross:** The cross reminds you that Jesus is the greatest gift ever given. He gave His life on the cross so you could live with Him forever. His life empowers you to overcome sin.
- **The Sword:** Just as the squire destroyed the dragon with his sword, you can defeat the Evil One by knowing and obeying the Sword of the Spirit, the Word of God.
- **The Lantern:** The lantern will remind you of who you are. Even if you do not feel like one at times, you are a Protector of the Purest Light. You are a Squire of the Lantern!
- **The Watch:** Time is very important to a young squire. This watch will remind you that it takes time to read and memorize God's Scroll to prepare you to become His knight.
- **The Scroll:** The scroll represents the Word of God. It will guide your life when you obey its truth and wisdom.

Shield and Lantern Watch

For more information or to purchase, contact:

Revive Our Hearts
P.O. Box 2000
Niles, MI 49120
1-800-569-5959
www.ReviveOurHearts.com/squire

Shield size: 37 mm x 47 mm

How can a young man keep his way pure? By living according to your word. Psalm 119:9 NIV